The Life and Times of

CONSTANTINE

Mitchell Lane
PUBLISHERS

P.O. Box 196
Hockessin, Delaware 19707

Titles
in the Series

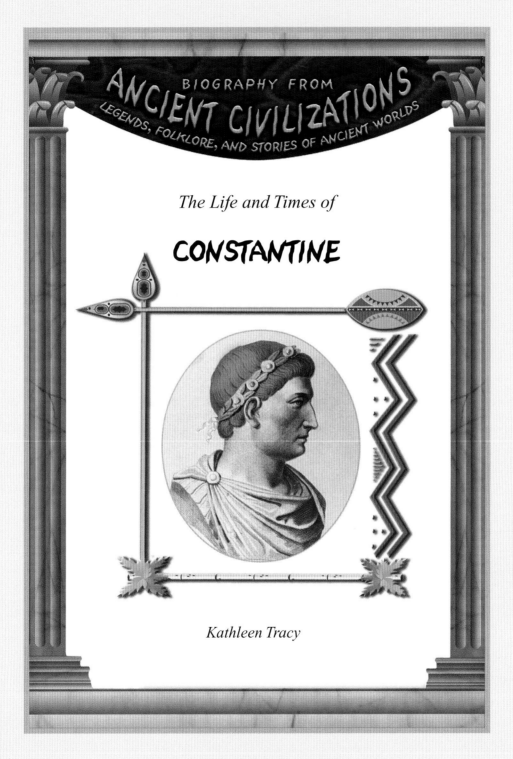

The Life and Times of

CONSTANTINE

Kathleen Tracy

Printing 1   2   3   4   5   6   7   8
Library of Congress Cataloging-in-Publication Data

Tracy, Kathleen.
    The life and times of Constantine / by Kathleen Tracy.
        p. cm. — (Biography from ancient civilizations)
    Includes bibliographical references and index.
    ISBN 1-58415-343-1 (library bound)
    1. Constantine I, Emperor of Rome, d. 337—Juvenile literature. 2. Emperors—Rome—Biography—Juvenile literature. 3. Rome—History—Constantine I, the Great, 306–337—Juvenile literature. 4. Church history—Primitive and early church, ca. 30–600—Juvenile literature. I. Title. II. Series.
DG315.T73   2005
937'.08—dc22
                                                                2004024416

ABOUT THE AUTHOR: Kathleen Tracy has been a journalist for over twenty years. Her writing has been featured in magazines including *The Toronto Star*'s "Star Week," *A Biography* magazine, *KidScreen* and *TV Times*. She is also the author of numerous biographies including, *The Boy Who Would be King* (Dutton), *Jerry Seinfeld—The Entire Domain* (Carol Publishing), *Don Imus—America's Cowboy* (Carroll), *Mariano Guadalupe Vallejo*, and *William Hewlett: Pioneer of the Computer Age* both for Mitchell Lane. Also for Mitchell Lane, she wrote *The Life and Times of Confucius* and *The Life and Times of Homer*. She recently completed *Diana Rigg: The Biography* for Benbella Books.

PHOTO CREDITS: Cover, pp. 1, 3, 34—Corbis; p. 6—Maquettes-Historiques/Le Grand Cirque; pp. 12, 18, 20, 28—Jamie Kondrchek; p. 26—Philadelphia Museum of Art/Corbis; p. 32—Web Gallery of Art; p. 36—Orthodox Church of America; p. 41—Roman Numismatic Gallery.

BIOGRAPHY FROM
ANCIENT CIVILIZATIONS
LEGENDS, FOLKLORE, AND STORIES OF ANCIENT WORLDS

The Life and Times of

CONSTANTINE

*For Your Information

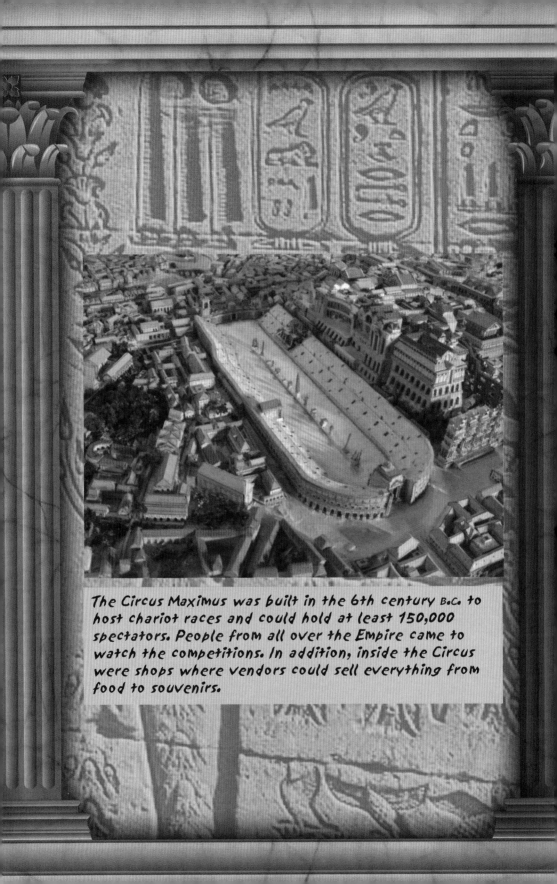

The Circus Maximus was built in the 6th century B.C. to host chariot races and could hold at least 150,000 spectators. People from all over the Empire came to watch the competitions. In addition, inside the Circus were shops where vendors could sell everything from food to souvenirs.

CHAPTER
ONE

ROME BURNS

During the reign of the Emperor Nero, the city of Rome was a sprawling metropolis with an estimated population of two million people living among the narrow roadways and densely packed neighborhoods. Sometime during the night of July 19, 64, a fire broke out on a street lined with shops near the Circus Maximus, the stadium where chariot races and other public entertainments were held. While fires weren't uncommon, this blaze spread with unusual speed. In a short time, it became an inferno burning out of control. Panicked residents watched in horror as the wall of flames rushed towards them. The Roman historian Tacitus (TAS-it-us)describes the chaos in *The Annals*: "When they escaped to a neighboring quarter, the fire followed. . . . Finally, with no idea where or what to flee, they crowded on to the country roads, or lay in the fields. Some who had lost everything . . . could have escaped but preferred to die. So did others, who had failed to rescue their loved ones. Nobody dared fight the flames."[1]

When the fire broke out, Nero was away from the city at his country home. By the time he returned to Rome, much of the city, including his palace, was in ruins. Even though Nero instituted emergency assistance to Rome's citizens, opening his private gardens as a temporary homeless shelter and bringing in food, rumors began to swirl that the Emperor himself may have been responsible for the devastating fire. Prior to the blaze, Nero had announced plans to tear down a third of Rome in order to build several palaces and call the new development Neropolis (near-AH-poe-lis). This grandiose scheme had been adamantly opposed by the Senate. Its members did not want Rome named after Nero. So as Rome burned, some people wondered if the Emperor had stage-managed the blaze so he could rebuild Rome as a monument to himself without Senate approval. That belief was furthered by Tacitus, who claimed "while the city was burning, Nero had gone on his private stage and, comparing modern calamities with ancient, had sung of the destruction of Troy."[2] He may have accompanied himself with a lyre, a stringed instrument similar to a small harp.

Few people doubted that Nero was capable of being so ruthless. After the sudden death of his stepfather Claudius (CLAW-dee-us) in 54, Nero became emperor when he was just 16 years old. It was widely believed that Nero's mother, Agrippina—who was also Claudius's wife—poisoned her husband with mushrooms so her son could assume the throne. At first, she exerted a great deal of influence on Nero. Since women could not hold political office, this was the only way for Agrippina (ag-ruh-PEE-nuh) to wield power.

It didn't take long for Nero's thirst for power and self-glorification to conflict with his mother's wishes. Like many young men, he probably wanted to get away from a domineering mother. Within a year or two, he rid himself of her influence.

Then he decided to rid himself of her entirely. After several blotched attempts to kill her, some of his men stabbed her to death in 59. Now he could rule the Empire as he wanted. Three years later, he killed his wife Octavia so he could marry another woman. If any Roman senators confronted Nero, they too were putting their lives at risk. Living under such a reign of terror, it's easy to see why people believed Nero had started the fire for his personal gain.

When the fire finally burned itself out nine days after it started, almost 70 percent of Rome had been destroyed. Upset at the rumors about his alleged involvement, Nero went on the offensive. He accused a then-obscure Jewish religious sect who called themselves Christians of setting the fire. Interestingly, some modern historians think Nero may have been right. Professor Gerhard Baudy of Germany's University of Konstanz claims that his research has uncovered evidence that in the first century, followers of Christ handed out warnings that an inferno would burn Rome to the ground. "In all of these oracles, the destruction of Rome by fire is prophesied," he explains. "That is the constant theme: Rome must burn. This was the long-desired objective of all the people who felt subjugated by Rome."[3]

Whether or not they had any involvement in igniting the fire, Christians had good reason to resent the Roman government. Christian converts tended to be among the city's poorest citizens or slaves. They were not allowed to practice their religion openly. If they were caught worshiping Christ, they could be executed for not worshiping the Emperor, who had proclaimed himself one of Rome's official gods. Even though nobody knows for sure how the great fire of Rome started or why it raged for so long, Christians paid for the disaster with their lives. Groups of Christians were rounded up and condemned to death without benefit of a trial.

Their executions would not be quick and merciful. In ancient Rome, capital punishment was a form of public entertainment, and the bloodier the better. Tacitus describes some of the brutal ways Christians were persecuted: "Dressed in wild animals' skins, they were torn to pieces by dogs, or crucified, or made into torches to be ignited after dark as substitutes for daylight. Nero provided his Gardens for the spectacle, and exhibited displays in the Circus, at which he mingled with the crowd. . . . Despite their guilt as Christians, and the ruthless punishment it deserved, the victims were pitied. For it was felt that they were being sacrificed to one man's brutality rather than to the national interest."[4]

Regardless of whatever sympathy some people might have felt for Christians at the hands of Nero, nobody intervened. But his brutality and ego had made him increasingly unpopular. Eventually, Rome's aristocrats, the Senate, and even his army turned against the Emperor. When the governor of Spain revolted against Nero and led an army to Rome to confront him in 68, Nero was forced to leave the majestic palace he had built for himself and flee Rome. Realizing he had lost his power, Nero stabbed himself to death. He was last in the line of rulers descended from the family of Julius Caesar and Augustus Caesar.

Nero's end was a relief to most Romans. To Christians, it marked the beginning of persecutions that would continue for more than two centuries. Then they would find a champion, and a convert, in the most unlikely of places.

Julius Caesar

Julius Caesar is one of the most important, and controversial, figures in Roman history. He was born into a prominent Roman family in 100 B.C. At the time, his uncle, Marius, was a very popular Roman leader. It seemed natural that Caesar would also be interested in politics. He was elected to public office in 65 B.C. where his job was to oversee public entertainment. Three years later he was elected to the position of *praetor*, which is somewhat like a modern-day judge.

Julius Caesar with some of his staff

Knowing that if he ever wanted true power he would have to prove himself on the battlefield, Caesar successfully waged a military campaign to conquer Gaul, which is now France. He was considered as a military genius and one of Rome's great generals.

Pompey, one of Caesar's rivals, was worried that Caesar might try to name himself supreme ruler of Rome. So he tried to have Caesar's army taken away. Instead, Caesar started a civil war and eventually ran Pompey out of Italy. By 49 B.C., Caesar had himself appointed consul, which was similar to our President. The public loved Caesar. But other Roman leaders were upset with how much power he had. Two former followers of Pompey, Brutus and Cassius, organized a plot to kill Caesar. They and more than twenty other men stabbed him to death on the floor of the Roman Senate on March 15, 44 B.C.

The reforms Caesar started would live on after his death. Today we can still see Caesar's influence. He is responsible for the Julian Calendar. Previously, the 12-month Roman calendar was only 355 days long. This meant that extra months would have to be periodically added to make the seasons match the months. For example, in 46 B.C., Caesar had to add four extra months. To correct this situation, he adjusted the calendar so there were 365.25 days. That meant there would be an extra day added every fourth year, which we now call leap year. He also changed the name of the seventh month, Quinctilis, to July in honor of himself.

Nero was one of the most feared and disliked
rulers in Roman history. When the great fire
broke out, it was rumored that Nero
celebrated by playing a musical instrument.
Nero had ascended to the thrown with the
help of his power-hungry mother, Agrippina.
But once he was ruler, Nero had his mother
killed, unwilling to share power with her.

CHAPTER
TWO

HUMBLE BEGINNINGS

Because the Roman Empire was so vast, the men who ruled it needed a large army to prevent invasions and to quell any uprisings by disgruntled citizens. The cost of running the army was paid for by each emperor, whose power depended upon the loyalty of his generals and their men. Soldiers were both volunteers and those conscripted, or drafted, into the military. They had to serve for terms of up to 25 years before they were eligible for retirement. Those who were fortunate enough to survive that long were given a bonus—a substantial cash payment or a gift of land.

While the average foot soldier had little opportunity for career advancement, officers were chosen by the emperor and enjoyed power and prestige. Many used their military service as a springboard into politics or other important positions. One such man was Flavius Constantius (FLAY-vee-us con-STAN-tee-us), who was posted in what today is Eastern Europe during the third century. The son of a farmer, Constantius grew up helping his father herd sheep and working the land until he joined the military. He quickly rose through the ranks and became a well-regarded commander.

Sometime—probably during 272 while on the way back from a military campaign—Flavius and his men pitched camp one night at the town of Naissus in modern-day Serbia. A local innkeeper introduced the dashing soldier to his teenage daughter, Helena, who worked in the tavern. Even though tavern girls were looked down upon by many people in the upper levels Roman society, Constantius was immediately attracted to the girl and they began a romantic relationship.

Sometime in either 273 or 274—historians disagree as to the year—Helena gave birth to a son. She named the boy Constantine, which means "Little Constantius." Despite having a child together, there is no record that Constantius ever married Helena, probably because of her low economic class. But at that time in Rome, it was quite acceptable for an important man to keep a mistress, a woman with whom he had a relationship outside of marriage. So Helena quietly raised their son while over the years Constantius became an important leader. He became governor of Dalmatia in 284 or 285, and many people thought he was destined for even higher offices.

At some point, Constantius probably brought Helena and the boy to Salonae, the capital of Dalmatia. For a boy like Constantine, moving from a rural area to the capital city of the province would have been a major adjustment.

One of the biggest differences was the opportunity for education. While the large cities had public schools, most children growing up in the country during the time of the Roman Empire did not attend school. Few rural families could afford a

Because they didn't have paper, Roman school children learned to write by using a pointed stick called a stylus on a wax tablet. To erase their work and start over, they would simply smooth out the wax with the flat end of the stylus.

tutor or to send their children to private schools. Those children could learn to read and write only if their parents were literate and could teach them at home.

However, children of aristocrats had many more opportunities. Being the son of a governor meant that Constantine now had the best private tutors to school him in a variety of subjects and skills including law, mathematics, and public speaking. He was coached in physical training in order to prepare him for the day he would join the military. Roman education also included being taught respect for law, obedience to authority, and honesty. These qualities were considered important to be a good citizen and a capable leader.

Instruction usually began shortly after sunrise and took up much of the day. Schoolchildren in Roman times did not have paper. To practice writing, they used a thin pointed metal device called a stylus to carve words into a wax tablet. To start over, all the student had to do was smooth over the wax with the flat end of the stylus. To learn mathematics, children used an *abacus*, a rectangular frame lined with columns of beads strung in sets of tens. A crossbar divided the beads into five above and five below.

A Roman hand abacus. The abacus was a device used to calculate both simple arithmetic and more complex mathematical problems. It was particularly important to traders, who used it to determine bookkeeping, and engineers who needed to figure out calculations for building roads and bridges.

The bead column furthest to the right represented ones, the second from the right represented tens and so on. By moving the beads in a certain way, students could solve basic math problems involving addition, subtraction, multiplication, and division with the accuracy of a modern-day calculator. The *abacus* could even be used to figure out square roots and cube roots.

Constantine proved to be a good student, studying hard to improve himself and to prepare himself for whatever opportunities came his way. Although there are hardly any details of his teenage years, it seems likely that he rarely saw his father, who was frequently off on military campaigns while pursuing his political ambitions. To further those ambitions, Constantius married a woman named Theodora a few years after he became the governor of Dalmatia. She was the daughter of Maximian, an important political leader. Constantius would eventually have six children with her.

By all accounts, the marriage to Theodora was more of a political strategy than a gesture of love. That strategy may have originated in 283 when Emperor Carus died suddenly during a military campaign in Persia. The official report given at the time was that he had been struck by lightning during a freak storm. But it is more likely he was killed by one of his generals who disagreed with Carus' military policies. The commander of Carus' personal guard, an ambitious man named Diocletian (dye-oh-KLEE-shun), was named Emperor a year later.

One of Diocletian's first acts was to dramatically change the way the Empire was governed. He decided that the Roman Empire was too big for just one man to rule. So he split it in half and named himself leader, or *Augustus*, of the eastern half and named Maximian *Augustus* of the western half—Gaul (modern-day France), Spain, and Britain. Several years later, Diocletian also appointed two *Caesars*, or junior "emperors in training," to ensure further stability. In the east, the *Caesar* was Galerius and in the west it was Constantius.

According to Michael DiMaio, Jr., "This arrangement, called the 'Tetrarchy,' was meant not only to provide a stronger foundation for the two emperors' rule but also to end any possible fighting over the succession of the throne once the two senior *Augusti* had left the throne—a problem which had bedeviled [leaders] since the time of the Emperor Augustus."[1]

In addition each member of the Tetrarchy—a word that literally means "four rulers"—would be headquartered in a different city, two in each half of the empire.

Now was the time when Constantius' marriage to Theodora paid off. It is likely that one reason for his selection as *Caesar* was that she was the daughter of the western *Augustus*. It helped to put him in line for the day when he would succeed his father-in-

In an effort to keep the transition of power peaceful, Diocletian established a system of leadership called the Tetrarchy. He split the Empire into eastern and western halves and named a supreme ruler, or Augustus, for east and west. Then he named a sub-leader, called a Caesar to be the Augustus-in-waiting. However, after the death of Constantine's father, the tetrarchy crumbled and Constantine ended up battling his rivals for the right to rule Rome.

law as co-*Augustus* of the Roman Empire. In turn, it put Constantine in the spotlight as a possible successor to his father.

Unlike the royal families of Europe, the title of emperor did not necessarily automatically pass from father to son. Many times, the position was taken by force or through violence. But even though Constantine was still in his early 20s, few people doubted that he was destined to follow in his father's footsteps and one day help rule the Roman Empire. What nobody could know was that Constantine was destined to become a leader who would not only change the Roman Empire but also the course of world's religious history.

Roman Social Classes

For Your Info

Roman history is divided into two eras: the Roman Republic and the Roman Empire. During the Republic, the Senate was the seat of political power. Since senators were all aristocrats, there was social tension with the lower classes, which had few rights and almost no input in the government.

After Rome started being ruled by an emperor, rules for the Senate changed. Over time, people from the lower classes won their fight for more equality and were eventually able to hold major political and religious positions. Despite these improved conditions, there were still clear-cut distinctions between classes of citizens during the Roman Empire.

Patricians were the aristocrats. They were wealthy landowners, who usually held the majority of political posts and were often wealthy businessmen. As was the case with latter-day European royal families, a person was usually born into a patrician family.

Plebeians were the ordinary citizens of Rome. They made up the vast majority of the population. While some plebeians were poor and homeless, many were successful small businessmen such as farmers, merchants, and artisans.

Slaves were an important part of the Empire's economy and social structure. In Roman times, slavery was not based on race or skin color but rather the power of the Roman army. Many people from areas captured in battle were sent back to Rome as slaves, where they performed all the manual labor. Well-educated slaves could also serve as doctors and teachers. Both patricians and plebeians owned slaves. Many slaves were paid a salary and some managed to buy their freedom. Others were simply given their freedom in appreciation for years of service. These former slaves were called freedmen.

Non-Roman citizens from newly conquered areas of the Empire were called barbarians.

While the social structure had been rigid during the Republic, it was possible for people to improve their social class as they became financially successful under conditions that existed during the Empire. Another change was that women—who had no rights during the Republic—could own property and run businesses on their own. These social and political advances helped stabilize the huge empire and allowed it to thrive for centuries despite containing so many diverse cultures.

To commemorate his victory at the Milvian Bridge in 312 A.D. over Maxentius, Constantine had an arch built in the center of Rome near the Coliseum. Standing over 60 feet high, the Arch of Constantine is ornately decorated with statues and reliefs and remains a popular tourist destination.

CHAPTER
THREE

COMING OF AGE

After Constantius was appointed *Caesar*, he spent several years waging military campaigns. In the summer of 293 he fought the troops of Carausius (Kare-AH-see-us), the ruler of Britain and part of Gaul, who had revolted against Rome. He controlled some unrest in Germany and in 296 crossed the English Channel to recapture Britain from Carausius's follower, Allectus. Between 300 and 305 Constantius further secured the frontier along the River Rhine, all the while earning the loyalty of his troops and the respect of the people he ruled.

Rather than fighting alongside his father in the West, Constantine was required to stay with the eastern *Caesar*, Galerius. Although the Tetrarchy was supposed to eliminate bloody coups by spreading the power throughout the Empire, there was still a certain amount of mistrust among its leaders. So to make sure that Constantius didn't stage a coup d'état, or overthrow, of the others, Constantine was kept in the east as a kind of hostage. In addition, Diocletian didn't want Constantine to assume he would take over his father's position.

Just as his father's reputation had grown with each victory, Constantine had also begun to earn a reputation of his own. He participated in Diocletian's Egyptian expedition in 296 and fought alongside Galerius in the Persian campaign the following year. Exceedingly popular among the soldiers in his command, Constantine already exuded the charisma of a born leader. According to Eusebius, a Christian who wrote *The Life of Constantine* in the early fourth century: "In handsome physique and bodily height no other could bear comparison with him; in physical strength he so exceeded his contemporaries as even to put them in fear; he took pride in moral qualities rather than physical superiority, ennobling his soul first and foremost with self-control, and thereafter distinguishing himself by the excellence of his rhetorical education, his instinctive shrewdness and his God-given wisdom."[1]

In 305, Diocletian's health began to fail from an eye infection he had contracted. Believing it was time to step down as the eastern Emperor, with some difficulty he convinced Maximian that they both should abdicate, or resign, at the same time. That meant that Constantius and Galerius would now become the co-emperors.

On May 1, 305, Diocletian, who was in Nicomedia (located in what is now Turkey), and Maximian in Milan, each officially stepped down as *Augustus* by removing their purple robes, the color worn only by the emperor. Constantius and Galerius took their place. Their rise to *Augustus* meant that two new *Caesars* had to be named.

"Everyone in Galerius' army expected Constantine . . . to be one of them, and there was great disappointment and surprise when this turned out not to be so,"[2] writes Michael Grant. The selections turned out to be Severus—a close friend of Galerius—and Galerius' nephew, Maximinus Daia.

Now that he was *Augustus*, Constantius insisted that his son be allowed to join him in the west. He argued that he needed Constantine's leadership and military knowledge to help in the campaign against the Picts, a fierce tribe in northern Scotland that was invading Britain. Unable to keep Constantine any longer, Galerius relented and let him leave. Eusebius also suggests that there might have been concern for Constantine's safety: "As a result of this those then in power observed with envy and fear that the young man was fine, sturdy and tall, full of good sense. They reckoned that his stay with them was not safe for them, and devised secret plots against him, though out of respect for his father they avoided inflicting public death upon him. The young man was aware of this . . . he sought safety in flight. . . ."[3]

Constantine was finally reunited with his father at the port city of Boulogne in Gaul in early 306. They crossed the English Channel together into Britain to put down the rebellion.

But Constantine's time with his father was fated to be brief. On July 25, 306 Constantius died at his residence in York, a town in Britain. According to some accounts, before he died Constantius named his son to be successor as emperor. Other stories say that when Constantius' troops learned he had died, they hailed Constantine as his replacement.

Constantine might have been ready to assume the purple robe. Galerius was not ready for that to happen. He appointed Severus to be the *Augustus* in the west. Constantine had to be content with being named as *Caesar*. But things got complicated a few months later when Maximian's son, Maxentius, seized Rome and proclaimed himself as *Augustus*. Suddenly, three men were laying claim to the west—Constantine, Severus, and Maxentius.

At Galerius' urging, Severus led an army to Rome to fight Maxentius the following year. In response, Maxentius convinced his father, the former *Augustus* Maximian, to come out of retirement. He offered him the purple robe in exchange for his help. Maximian probably didn't need much convincing. He had only given up his high position because Diocletian had asked him to. Maximian proved his value right away by helping to persuade many of the men in Severus' army to defect to their side. The plan worked, forcing Severus to flee with the few soldiers who had not defected. Maximian convinced Severus to surrender after promising him he would not be harmed. Meanwhile, Galerius organized his own army and prepared to invade Italy to fight Maximian and restore Severus as *Augustus*. But he failed. Severus was soon put to death.

Maximian and Maxentius were still afraid of Galerius. They appealed to Constantine for help. To seal the deal, he married Fausta, the sister of Maxentius. He had been under some pressure to marry her more than a decade earlier. At that time, he had decided to marry a woman named Minervina. But she had been dead for some time.

Throughout the turmoil, Constantine also continued to lay claim to the *Augustus* title. For several years, the western half of the empire remained unsettled. Maximian and Maxentius soon had a falling out. Maximian fled to Constantine. But the two men didn't get along. In 310, Maximian tried to overthrow Constantine. He failed, and hanged himself. During this time, bad blood continually boiled between Maxentius and Constantine. It was only a matter of time before there would be a confrontation.

That showdown finally happened in 312 when Maxentius initiated plans to invade Gaul, where Constantine had his headquarters. Constantine knew it was time to take action. Unwilling to wait for Maxentius to attack him, Constantine went on the offensive and marched his army across the Alps into northern Italy, where he defeated Maxentius' forces twice. The rest of Maxentius' army was waiting for Constantine in front of the Milvian Bridge, which was on a road just outside of Rome. Whoever won the upcoming battle would be the emperor of the west.

According to Lactantius, a Christian who tutored Constantine's son and would later become an important historian, Constantine had a dream on the evening of October 27 as both armies prepared for battle. According to the dream, he was ordered to place the sign of the Christian cross on the shields of his men before they marched into battle. At the time, he believed in the Roman gods, so this was a major step for him to take.

When Eusebius wrote about the battle 25 years later, his version was somewhat different. According to him, as Constantine and his men were marching to confront Maxentius, they all saw the Greek letters Chi and Rho—the first two letters of "Christ" in Greek—written on a fiery cross visible in the sun, along with the inscription *In Hoc Signo Vinces*, which is Latin for "Under this sign, you will conquer." Then the next night, according to Eusebius, Christ appeared to Constantine in a vision and instructed him to put the cross on his battle standards.

After the death of his father, Constantine set out to be the leader of Rome and led his army in battle against rival leaders. His victory at the Battle of Milvian Bridge would establish Constantine as sole ruler of Rome and set into motion social and religious changes that would forever alter the course of human history.

Whatever the inspiration was—dream or vision or intuition—Constantine put the symbol of the cross on his soldiers' shields. This standard would later become known in Latin as the *labarum*.

The next day, the two armies met in a furious battle. Despite being outnumbered, Constantine soon had Maxentius' soldiers on the run. Maxentius tried to retreat. But the only way back to Rome was over the bridge, which impeded his escape. He was killed and the battle was over. When Constantine marched victoriously into Rome, he was unanimously acclaimed as the sole western *Augustus*. The Senate voted to construct the Arch of Constantine in his honor. Still standing, it is the largest triumphal arch in Rome and contains the phrase, "Constantine overcame his enemies by divine inspiration."

Constantine's victory at the Milvian Bridge not only changed the balance of power in the Empire, but it also put into motion a spiritual revolution that would bring Christianity into the Roman mainstream.

Eusebius

Much of what we know about the early history of the church is based on the historical writings of Eusebius of Caesarea. Although no one can be completely positive where or when he was born, it was probably around A.D. 260 in Palestine.

Eusebius

As an adult, he first met the future emperor when Constantine visited Palestine in A.D. 296 with Diocletian. A devout man with a strong desire to study and learn, Eusebius became acquainted with a well-known priest and theologian named Pamphilius, with whom he studied the Bible. In fact, they became so close Eusebius is also frequently called Eusebius Pamphili, which in Latin means "Eusebius, the friend of Pamphilus."

Eventually Eusebius was appointed bishop of Caesarea in Palestine around 313 and became increasingly active in church politics. By the time he attended the Council of Nicaea, a gathering in 325 of three hundred church leaders whose goal was to unify differing factions of the young Church, he was already a well-known and respected historian. He is associated with the development of the Nicene Creed. The Creed is a statement of religious belief that is a part of most Christian Church services today. Among his other works are a history of the martyrs of Palestine and a collection of religious prophesies, or predictions.

His two most important achievements are the Ecclesiastical History, a history of the church that details the evolution of Christianity from an outlaw religion to the official faith of the Roman Empire, and the biography *Life of Constantine*.

Although some modern historians have suggested that Eusebius may have been biased toward Constantine in his biography of the Emperor—showcasing his achievements and downplaying or ignoring altogether his more brutal acts—by and large the actual content of his works is considered to be accurate. Eusebius paid meticulous attention to documenting his sources when excerpting from other works of his day—many of which have been lost over the centuries—and this has given his writing validity and helped it stand the test of time.

When Octavia, the grand-nephew of Julius Caesar, became the first Emperor of Rome, he was given the name Augustus, which means "the exalted." Under his reign Rome enjoyed great prosperity and peace. He ordered thousands of miles of roads built, established a postal system, encouraged trade, and funded the arts. When he died, Romans worshipped him as a god.

CHAPTER
FOUR

CONSTANTINE'S CONVERSION

For average Romans, religion played an important part in their daily lives. They believed there were many gods. Each god controlled different aspects of the world, from oceans and rivers to falling in love. Jupiter was the king of the gods along with his wife Juno, who was the goddess of women and marriage. But after the time of Emperor Augustus, who ruled from 27 B.C. to 14 A.D., emperors were officially considered gods, too. Not everyone really believed this to be the case, but by law they were required to act as if they did.

For some leaders, any religion that did not conform to traditional Roman beliefs was intolerable. Part of the reasoning was that since the emperors ruled by "divine right," disbelief in the Roman gods could undermine the authority of the emperor. Galerius in particular firmly believed that Christians, whose numbers seemed to be growing, were a danger to the empire. So during the period that Diocletian was emperor, Galerius convinced him that something needed to be done to thwart Christianity. In 303, Diocletian initiated a royal edict requiring everyone to offer sacrifices to the Roman gods.

In his *Ecclesiastical History*, as Eusebius recounts, "Royal edicts were published everywhere, commanding that the churches should be razed to the ground, the Scriptures destroyed by fire, those who held positions of honor degraded, and the household servants, if they persisted in the Christian profession, be deprived of their liberty."[1]

A year later, Galerius himself issued an edict that was even harsher. Eusebius writes that according to the new proclamation, "rulers of the churches in every place should be first put in prison and afterwards compelled by every device to offer sacrifice. . . . Then as the first decrees were followed by others commanding that those in prison should be set free, if they would sacrifice, but that those who refused should be tormented with countless tortures."[2]

When Galerius became senior emperor after Diocletian stepped down, he increased his attacks on Christians. His effort to wipe out Christianity was so widespread and so violent that it became known as the Great Persecution. Known church leaders were put in prison, New Testament manuscripts were destroyed, and thousands of people were martyred, or executed, for their faith when they refused to offer sacrifice to the Roman gods. But to Galerius' frustration, the persecution only seemed to make Christians more resolute in their beliefs.

In 311, Galerius fell seriously ill and had an abrupt change of heart. He feared that his deteriorating health and the agonizing pain he suffered was a punishment from the Christian God. Desperate to recover, he issued the Edict of Toleration, which was aimed only at Christians. Other religions were not included.

The edict began by trying to explain the reason for the persecution. As Galerius said, "Amongst our other measures for the advantage of the Empire, we have hitherto endeavored to bring all things into conformity with the ancient laws and public order of the Romans. We have been especially anxious that even the Christians, who have abandoned the religion of their ancestors, should return to reason. . . . Nevertheless, since many of them have continued to persist in their opinions . . . we, with our wonted [according to habit] clemency, have judged it wise to extend a pardon even to these men and permit them once more to become Christians and reestablish their places of meeting; in such manner, however, that they shall in no way offend against good order. . . . Wherefore it should be the duty of the Christians, in view of our clemency, to pray to their god for our welfare, for that of the Empire, and for their own, so that the Empire may remain intact in all its parts, and that they themselves may live safely in their habitations."[3]

If Galerius had hoped that Christians praying for him would help him recover, he was fatally disappointed. Just a week after issuing the edict, he died.

Most of these persecutions had taken place in the eastern half of the empire. On coming to power, Constantine had ended all persecutions in the territories he ruled, even though he still believed in the Roman gods. But that belief changed after his experience prior to the Battle of the Milvian Bridge. Convinced that his victory against Maxentius had happened with help from the Christian God, Constantine converted and committed himself to the new religion. Around this time, Constantine's mother, Helena, reappears in historical accounts. She, too, had converted to Christianity and became an important part of the emperor's inner circle.

According to legend, the night before Constantine was to fight Maxentius' army at the Milvian Bridge he dreamt that to ensure a victory he should put the Christian cross on the shields of all his soldiers. After defeating Maxentius, Constantine converted to Christianity, believing his dream was a sign from God.

Around February 313, Constantine attended the wedding between his half-sister Constantia and Licinius, the emperor in the east. During their time together, Constantine convinced Licinius it was to his political advantage to agree to a new religious policy that would apply to the entire Roman Empire. Known as the Edict of Milan, the new policy made Christianity legal and ordered all persecutions to stop.

But Licinius eventually reneged on his promise and started persecuting Christians again. Many historians believe that

Constantine had been waiting for a reason to fight Licinius, with whom he had a strained relationship. These strains probably were inevitable. In the end, both men wanted to assume the sole power for governing the empire. A confrontation was inevitable after Constantine claimed to have discovered a plot engineered by Licinius to assassinate him.

In 316, Constantine and Licinius went to war. At a battle in modern-day Hungary, Constantine's army inflicted heavy casualties on Licinius' men. After a second battle, the two men reached an agreement. Licinius had to give up all the European provinces he had previously ruled. That moved the border dividing the two parts of the empire substantially further to the east.

But the truce did not hold, in large part because of the two men's different policies on religion. They declared war on each other in 324 and once again Constantine's army defeated Licinius. But this time, Constantine stripped Licinius of all his power and eventually ordered his execution. Constantine also ordered the death of Licinius' son. Constantine was now the undisputed emperor of the entire Roman world.

Just two months after defeating Licinius, Constantine's major first act as supreme emperor was to begin the creation of a new capital for the empire. He chose the ancient Greek city of Byzantium, which lay along the traditional trade route that linked the Black Sea with the Mediterranean. He changed its name to Nova Roma (New Rome) and laid out new boundaries that quadrupled the city's size.

Constantine personally oversaw some of the construction, and put pressure on architects and builders to work as fast as

Constantinople was originally founded in 667 B.C. by Greek colonists who named the city Byzantium. When taken over by the Romans in 196 A.D., the city suffered extensive damage but was rebuilt by the Roman Emperor Severus. Constantinople remained the capital of the East Roman Empire from the time Constantine renamed it in 330 until it fell to the Turks in 1453.

possible. In four years, the walls surrounding the city were completed, and on May 11, 330 the city was formally dedicated.

In many ways, New Rome—or Constantinople, as it soon became known—resembled old Rome both in appearance and function. Like Rome, it was built on seven hills. There was a senate and the government subsidized citizens with food. Residents of the city gathered at the Hippodrome, a large race track that was also a social center of the city. But there were also stark differences. Instead of monuments and statues honoring the Roman gods, Constantine began constructing churches, making it clear he believed that Constantinople was not just the capital of the empire but the capital of Christianity as well.

The Rise of Christianity

Christianity started as a movement within Judaism by Jews who believed Jesus Christ was the Messiah who had been foretold in the Old Testament. Other Jews merely thought Christ was a prophet, or special messenger, from God.

Most authorities assumed that after the crucifixion of Jesus, his followers would disband and the movement would fade away. But the religion was kept alive by enthusiastic believers. As time went on, Christians separated themselves from Judaism. They considered themselves to be following a new religion, based on the belief that Christ had been the son of God. They tried to convert as many people as they could to their new religion. The most influential Christian in those early days was Paul of Tarsus, known today as Saint Paul.

SAINT PAUL

Ironically, Paul was a devout Jew who initially tried to suppress Christianity. But he converted to the new faith after a vision he had while traveling to the city of Damascus. He claimed to have seen the risen-from-the-dead Christ. Paul became a tireless missionary. He traveled throughout Greece and Turkey spreading the word of Christ and converting as many people as he could. He was one of the first to specifically seek out non-Jews to welcome into the new faith.

At the time it was official Roman policy to recognize many gods. Christians were adamant that there was only one God. They were intolerant of anyone who believed differently. The authorities considered them to be in violation of Roman law, which advanced tolerance of all religions. With an empire so vast, different regions would follow different faiths. To single out one religion ran the risk of upsetting large numbers of citizens and threatening the religious peace the Roman Empire had enjoyed for so long. As a result, many Roman leaders believed it was for the good of the Empire to persecute Christians to wipe out the potential dangers their religion posed.

These persecutions, such as the one mounted by Diocletian, failed. Over time, most Roman leaders began to accept Christianity as more and more citizens of the Empire embraced it.

To address religious differences among Christians, Constantine organized a meeting called the Council of Nicaea where Bishops, called the Fathers of the Ecumenical, settled the disputes.

CHAPTER
FIVE

A LASTING LEGACY

Constantine was not only responsible for running the empire. He also frequently found himself trying to resolve disputes within the Christian church, which had begun to develop factions. Even before he became sole emperor, he became involved in their disputes.

One such dispute involved the Donatists in North Africa. During the Great Persecution, many Christians there had been willing martyrs, refusing to try to hide their faith. Others, however, had renounced their beliefs publicly to avoid execution. Certain bishops, such as Caecilian in Carthage, canceled services and handed over scriptures. These actions reflected their belief that the lives of individual Christians were more important than manuscripts. But this behavior infuriated the hard-liners who refused to deny their God. These militant Christians called themselves Donatists, after a bishop named Donatus. He had spent six years in jail and endured the agonies of being put on the rack several times, yet refused to abandon his faith.

After the persecutions ended, the Donatists did not want anyone who had, at least in their eyes, betrayed Christ to be allowed back in the church. They also wanted any bishop who had handed over scriptures to be stripped of his position. Donatus accused Caecilian of being an illegal bishop and wanted to replace him.

To try to resolve the bitter conflict, Constantine ordered a council to convene in August 314 to hear from both sides. Constantine felt that the Donatists were too radical and rigid. He sided with the moderates who had avoided persecution. Unwilling to accept the decision, the Donatists split off from the main church and wielded considerable power in North Africa over the next several centuries.

Another dispute arose between two other Christian sects, the Arians and the Athanasians. The Arians, who followed the teachings of a priest named Arius, believed that since there was only one God, Jesus was not equal to God. The Athanasians, the followers of Athanasius who would later be the bishop of Alexandria, believed that there was absolutely no difference between Jesus and God in their divinity. This dispute led to bitter confrontations and forced Constantine to call for another meeting in 318 to resolve the issue. Although Arius' teachings were rejected and he was excommunicated, the dispute continued.

In 325, Constantine convened the Council of Nicaea, which has also become known as the First Ecumenical Council. At that gathering, Athanasius' view was reaffirmed and the council formulated a statement based on the belief that Christ and God are "of the same substance." Called the Nicene Creed, it still remains the fundamental statement of faith for Christians. Even though most of the bishops attending the council signed the creed, the disagreement over the nature of Christ's divinity would continue for years to come.

Despite his conversion, Constantine was still capable of some stunning cruelties. Not even his family was safe. His wife Fausta may have blamed Constantine for being responsible for the deaths of her brother and father and sought revenge. By the time that Constantine became the sole emperor, he and Fausta had three sons. She may have wanted to see them in power. The main obstacle was Crispus, Constantine's eldest son and his one child with Minervina. Crispus had already achieved a formidable reputation, helping his father win several battles.

In 326, Fausta made accusations against Crispus. Some historians believe that these charges involved Crispus making inappropriate advances toward her. Outraged, Constantine ordered Crispus to be executed. He was subsequently horrified when Helena revealed that Fausta's charges against Crispus had been lies. A short time later, Fausta was executed—either by forcible drowning in a bath of boiling water or by being locked inside an overheated steam room in a public bath. The names of both Fausta and Crispus were permanently erased from official records.

Shortly after this family tragedy, Helena took a pilgrimage to the Holy Land to visit the places where Christ had lived and died. While there she oversaw the building of two churches, one in Bethlehem near where Mary had given birth to Jesus and another near Jerusalem on the place where Christians believed Jesus had ascended into heaven. She was also active in helping the poor. One legend surrounding Helena is that she found the cross upon which Christ had been crucified. Because of her devout faith and good works, Helena was revered as a saint after her death in 330. Constantine honored his mother by having her body sent to Rome and buried in the tomb of the emperors. He also built a monument for her in the town where she had been born and changed its name to Helenopolis.

In his waning years as emperor, Constantine continued to leave his mark on the empire. Among his legacies was to establish a new currency, a gold coin called a *solidus*, which would be used for the next several centuries. One of the legal codes he established would have a long-lasting impact. It required tenant farmers to pay rent to the landowner, or lord, of the land they cultivated. In essence this tied the farmer to the land and the lord. This law turned the farmers into serfs and this system would lay the foundation for European society in the Middle Ages.

Although Constantine never outlawed pagan beliefs, as time went on, he pushed them more and more to the side as he made Christianity the official religion of the Roman Empire. Temples dedicated to Jupiter and other gods were torn down on his orders and ancient treasures were seized. During the tenth anniversary celebration of being named sole emperor, Constantine completely omitted all sacrifices to the Roman gods. His policies helped Christianity thrive without fear of persecution. But they also had the unfortunate consequence of fostering anti-Jewish sentiments and policies, which in turn would lay the foundation for medieval persecution of Jews.

Shortly after Easter in 337, Constantine fell ill. Sensing that he was dying, he traveled to Helenopolis and prayed at the tomb of Helena's favorite saint, the martyr Lucian, who had been imprisoned for nine years during the Great Persecution before

One of the many innovations Constantine initiated was a new gold coin, called the solidus, *which became the standard form of currency for several centuries. Just as we put the pictures of former Presidents on our bills and coins, Romans would honor leaders by engraving their portraits on the* solidus. *Pictured here is Constantine's son, Constantine II.*

being killed. Afterwards, Constantine went to Nicomedia where he was baptized. There was a reason for waiting so long. By accepting baptism so late in life, he believed that he would die without any sins.

It was an impressive ceremony. According to T. G. Elliot's *The Christianity of Constantine the Great*, "After receiving the sacrament on Ascension Day he put aside forever his imperial purple, and, in the white of a neophyte lay down on a white couch, and thanked God for His blessings. To his generals, who came to him in tears, he declared that he was now in possession of true life, and in a hurry to go to God."[1]

Soon afterward—within a few days or even a few hours—Constantine died, still wearing the white robes of his baptism.

To many people, Constantine was a paradox. He could be ruthless with his enemies but was a fierce protector of the persecuted. He embraced Christianity yet could kill in cold blood. But what he will be remembered for most was his devotion to his empire and his conviction for his adopted religion, which together created a legacy that continues to live on to this day.

FYI
For Your Info

Roman Engineering

The public bath house in which Fausta may have met her end is one example of the Roman talent for engineering, for which they seemed to have an innate ability. Their system for heating these facilities, which kept the water at a constant temperature without benefit of electricity, is still considered a technological wonder. The Romans were also the first civilization to develop expertise in bridge building, which was made possible by their ingenious use of the arch as a support system.

They built hundreds of miles of aqueducts to bring fresh water to the city of Rome. By some estimates, these aqueducts brought in more than 200 million gallons a day for public toilets, the public baths, and more than one thousand public fountains. Wealthy Romans even had aqueducts that brought water directly to their homes. This fresh water, combined with an advanced sewage system and regular garbage collection, gave Rome a level of hygiene almost unheard of in ancient times. Better hygiene meant fewer diseases, which helped the city flourish.

While the Romans may have been resented as an invading force in their far-flung territories, one of the lasting legacies of the Empire was the improvements in living conditions the Romans made to the lands they ruled. Accepting Roman rule became much easier when it brought state of the art technology with it to improve the quality of life.

The first thing Roman forces did after conquering an area was to build stone roads and brick and mortar bridges to make travel and communication with Rome easier and to link the colonies together with each other. The old saying "All roads lead to Rome" is based in fact because every road built did lead there. An advanced road system also increased trade, which helped outlying provinces prosper economically. In all, over 50,000 miles of roads were built.

Puente Alcantara

Roman building techniques were so advanced that many structures they built still stand, such as the Puente Alcantara, a bridge in Spain. It reaches a height of 164 feet and is 600 feet long, with each of the individual spans approaching 100 feet in length.

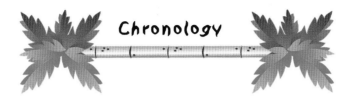

Chronology

273	Born in Naissus in present-day Serbia
296	Participates in Egyptian military campaign with Diocletian
306	Is named western emperor by his troops after his father's death
307	Marries Maximian's daughter Fausta
312	Defeats Maxentius at Milvian Bridge; converts to Christianity
313	Issues Edict of Milan, granting legal rights to all Christians
321	Declares Sunday as the official Christian Sabbath day
324	Defeats Licinius and becomes sole Roman emperor
325	Organizes Council of Nicaea
330	Builds Saint Peter's Basilica on the cemetery where Peter is buried
330	Dedicates the city of Constantinople (modern-day Istanbul, Turkey) as capital of the Roman Empire
333	Orders Christian Jews to sever all ties to Judaism under threat of death
337	Dies at the age of 63 in Nicodemia

Timeline in History

54	Nero becomes the emperor of Rome.
68	Nero commits suicide.
164	Rome suffers an outbreak of the plague, which kills an estimated one-tenth of the city's population.
200	Lemons are introduced into southern Italy.
247	Rome celebrates the thousandth anniversary of its founding.
284	Diocletian becomes Roman Emperor.
285	The religion of Confucianism is introduced to Japan.
300	The population of the Roman Empire reaches 60 million, 15 million of whom are Christians.
303	Diocletian orders persecution of Christians and destruction of their churches.
306	The Synod of Elvira prohibits marriage between Christians and Jews.
325	The first iron foundry is built in Britain.
350	The Codex Vaticanus, the first complete Bible, is written.
352	The first verified year that Christmas was celebrated on December 25.
376	Goths and other barbarians invade the Roman Empire.
380	Emperor Theodosius declares Christianity as the official state religion of the Roman Empire.
393	Theodosius abolishes the ancient Greek Olympics after more than 1,100 years because they are a pagan ritual.
395	The Roman Empire is divided into two portions, western and eastern.
476	The Roman Empire in the west falls and the Dark Ages begin.
570	Mohammed, the founder of the religion of Islam, is born.

Chapter Notes

CHAPTER ONE   ROME BURNS

1. Tacitus, *The Annals of Imperial Rome*, translated by Michael Grant (New York: Dorset Press, 1984), p. 363.

2. Ibid.

3. http://www.pbs.org/wnet/secrets/case_rome/clues.html

4. Tacitus, pp. 365-66.

5. Janeen Renaghan, "Savage Fashion: Animals and Attitude in Ancient Rome," *ZooGoer*, July–August, 1998.

6. Ibid.

CHAPTER TWO   HUMBLE BEGINNINGS

1. DiMaio, Michael Jr. An Online Encyclopedia of Roman Emperors. http://www.roman-emperors.org/conniei.htm

CHAPTER THREE   COMING OF AGE

1. Eusebius, *Life of Constantine*, translated by Averil Cameron and Stuart G. Hall (Oxford, United Kingdom: Clarendon Press, 1999), p. 77.

2. Michael Grant, *Constantine the Great* (New York: Charles Scribner's Sons, 1993), p. 21.

3. Eusebius, p. 78.

CHAPTER FOUR   CONSTANTINE'S CONVERSION

1. Eusebius, *Ecclesiastical History*, Book VIII, Chapter 2. http://www.acs.ucalgary.ca/~vandersp/Courses/texts/eusebius/eusehe8.html

2. Ibid.

3. http://www.pnna.org/pan/galerius.html

CHAPTER FIVE   A LASTING LEGACY

1. T. G. Elliot, *The Christianity of Constantine the Great* (Scranton, PA: University of Scranton Press, 1996), p. 325.

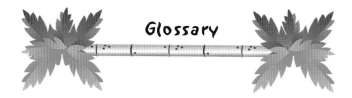
Glossary

abdicate	(AB-dih-cate)—to give up being king, queen, emperor, or other high position.
aqueduct	(A-kwuh-duct)—a structure designed to transport water from a remote source, usually by gravity.
Arianism	(AIR-een-uhn-izm)—an alternate belief from the generally accepted Christian teaching about the nature of the Holy Trinity. It was named after Arius, a priest in Alexandria, Egypt.
artisan	(ARE-tuh-zuhn)—a skilled craftsman, such as a blacksmith or cobbler.
Augustus	(uh-GUS-tus)—a Latin term that means "majestic" or "revered" and which came to be used to identify Roman emperors.
conscription	(cuhn-SCRIP-shun)—a system of compulsory recruitment for military service; a draft.
convert	(cuhn-VERT)—to adopt a new religion or system of beliefs.
dowry	(DOW-ree)—Money or valuables, including property, that the family of a bride is expected to present to her new husband upon marriage.
emperor	(EM-puhr-uhr)—one who rules an empire; an emperor can inherit the throne or can take it by military or political force.
heresy	(HAIR-uh-see)—going against common theory or practice, especially in matters of religion.
patricians	(puh-TRIH-shuns)—name given to Roman aristocrats.
pilgrimage	(PILL-gruh-midge)—a journey to a holy place or place of worship.
plebeians	(plih-BEE-uns)—name given to the Roman lower classes.

For Further Reading

For Young Adults

Malam, John and Mike Stuart Foster. *The Travelers Guide to Ancient Rome*. New York: Scholastic, 2001.

Morgan, Julian. *Constantine: Ruler of Christian Rome* (Leaders of Ancient Rome). New York: Rosen Publishing Group, 2002.

Nardo, Don. *Rulers of Ancient Rome*. San Diego, CA: Lucent Books, 1999.

Works Consulted

Elliott, T. G. *The Christianity of Constantine the Great*. Scranton, PA: University of Scranton Press, 1996.

Eusebius. *Life of Constantine*. Translated by Averil Cameron and Stuart G. Hall. Oxford, United Kingdom: Clarendon Press, 1999.

Grant, Michael. *Constantine the Great*. New York: Charles Scribner's Sons, 1993.

Kousoulas, D. G. *The Life and Times of Constantine the Great: The First Christian Emperor*. Poughkeepsie, NY: Netsource Distribution Services, 1997.

Tacitus. *The Annals of Imperial Rome*. Translated by Michael Grant. Publisher: Penguin Books. Place of Publication: London. Publication Year: 1963.

On the Internet

Gruen, Erich S. "Constantine the Great." World Book Online Reference Center. 2004. World Book, Inc.
http://www.aolsvc.worldbook.aol.com/wb/Article?id=ar130820

Sinnigen, William G. "Nero." World Book Online Reference Center. 2004. World Book, Inc.
http://www.aolsvc.worldbook.aol.com/wb/Article?id=ar387020

Secrets of the Dead: The Great Fire of Rome – PBS
http://www.pbs.org/wnet/secrets/case_rome/clues.html

The Internet Classic Archives – The Annals by Tacitus
http://classics.mit.edu/Tacitus/annals.html

An Online Encyclopedia of Roman Emperors
http://www.roman-emperors.org/conniei.htm

New Advent
http://www.newadvent.org/cathen/04295c.htm

The Influence of Roman Engineering and Architecture
http://www.arch.mcgill.ca/prof/sijpkes/arch304/winter2001/cszasz/u1/roman.htm

Rome Exposed – Marriage and Customs and Married Women
http://www.classicsunveiled.com/romel/html/marrcustwom.html

Index